Why my home did not sell?

WWW.SOLDBYCARRASCO.COM

Copyright © 2018 Luis Carrasco
All rights reserved.
ISBN: 9781730712371

WWW.SOLDBYCARRASCO.COM

FOR MY WIFE,

PEDAZO, THANK YOU FOR SUPPORTING ME

I LOVE YOU!!

CONTENTS

	Introduction	viii
	Disclaimer	ix
1	Why are you selling	Pg 1
2	Cleaning your home	Pg 4
3	Repairs, Upgrades & Additions	Pg 6
4	Curb Appeal	Pg 9
5	Staging Your Home	Pg 11
6	Disclosures	Pg 13
7	Fair Housing	Pg 15
8	Pricing Your Home	Pg 16
9	Type of Listings	Pg 20
10	Showing Your Property	Pg 23

WWW.SOLDBYCARRASCO.COM

11	Marketing Your Property	Pg 26
12	Choosing an Offer	Pg 29
13	Understanding the Contract	Pg 31
14	Condominium Sales	Pg 38
15	Land Sales	Pg 42
16	Selling & Buying Simultaneously	Pg 49
17	Seller Vs Buyer's Market	Pg 52
18	Why my property did not sell?	Pg 54
	Glossary	Pg 58
	About the Author	Pg 67

WWW.SOLDBYCARRASCO.COM

Introduction

When my wife and I, first listed our own home to sell, I did not have a Real Estate license at the time. I was unaware of how the selling process worked. I did not know what repairs or upgrades would make our home more appealing to the buyers. The failure to sell our home left us frustrated and unsure why our property did not sell.

This book is my way of giving sellers a basic guide on what to look when selling your home. The main goal of this book is to help you understand why your property did not sell. It will also help you in comprehending negotiations and being in the loop throughout the selling process. While real estate is littered with unexpected delays and potential deal breakers at each turn of the transaction, being prepared will help improve your chances of having a successful sale of your property.

If you live in the Phoenix Metro area, and are interested in a personal and custom analysis of why your home did not sell, feel free to contact me directly at:

Luis Carrasco
Re/Max Professionals
REALTOR
soldbycarrasco@gmail.com
(602) 643-8224

WWW.SOLDBYCARRASCO.COM

Disclaimer

This book is not legal advice. It is intended to provide you with the basic essential concepts of selling a home. Every home selling scenario is different, and the reader should seek legal counsel from their attorney or clarification from their Real Estate Agent in regards to real estate questions or concerns.

x

WWW.SOLDBYCARRASCO.COM

Chapter 1

WHY ARE YOU SELLING?

Before you start thinking of a price or choosing an agent; this is the first question that you need to answer. The answer will drive your listing strategy, contract negotiations and overall decision making during the sale process.

Common reasons for selling
There are many types of sellers and behind every one of them there are different motivations.

Downsizing Sellers
There are many reasons why homeowners look to downsize, it might due to their sons or daughters leaving the nest, and having a large house is not a priority anymore. Another reason might be to lower utilities cost, taxes etc. Usually the bigger the home, the higher the upkeep and maintenance costs.

Upgrading Sellers
Homeowners might be looking to buy their dream house, and they might use the equity towards the new home. The seller needs to

establish if they are looking to sell and buy simultaneously or they are planning to rent a place while they look for their new home.

Job relocation Sellers

Homeowners need to consider whether they want to rent the home or sell it. Both options have its pros and cons. If the seller is still making payments, he/she needs to determine how long can they carry the financial burden of making payments on their home and on their new place.

Financial problems

Homeowners with financial issues, might use their built-in equity to liquidate their financial obligations or simply eliminate the mortgage payments that might be a financial burden for the household. Sellers going thru financial issues, need to establish a timeline to sell their home.

Short time investors/ Flippers

These sellers are looking for selling their home at the shortest time possible and maximum price. They are educated sellers, very well aware that every month that goes by, they need to pay mortgage interest thereby lowering their profits. These sellers have time working against them, every day that goes by, it's a dollar less in profit.

Long term investors

These types of sellers have a long-term outlook of the market and are very practical in their decision making. Common issues with these sellers are properties with tenants in place and lease terms.

As-is condition sellers

They are not looking to spend any money or effort in making their home more appealing. They should expect to be flexible on offers received and factor in the home condition when pricing their home.

Proactive sellers
These types of sellers are proactive in getting their home in tip top shape to bring in the most money. They are willing to address repairs needed, before listing their property.

Every home seller is different, and they won't fit perfectly into these types. What matters is that you identify as much as possible your reasons behind the decision to sell and work with your agent to come up with strategy that suit your needs.

Chapter 2

CLEANING YOUR HOME

There's no greater feeling than having a clean home, and for a buyer this is no different. Do a one-time deep cleaning of your home, and when you have a showing do a quick clean. The following is a checklist of the most common cleaning tasks you can do to increase your home's appeal.

- Get rid of clutter to make the space look larger
- Clean the backyard, trim weeds, remove clutter
- Clean the bathrooms
- Wash all the windows if possible
- Pack up and store away all large pots and pans, it will make your cabinets look bigger
- Clean refrigerator, even if it's not included in the sale
- Shampoo carpets
- Clean light fixtures and switches
- Dust cobwebs
- Wash all rugs and mats
- Keep kitchen counter tops clean
- Clean stove inside and out
- Wipe down cabinets

- Clean baseboards
- Clean microwave

Cleaning tips for showing days

Every time you show your property, you need to make a positive first impression. Follow these quick tips to make your home show better.

- Wipe down countertops
- Keep fresh fruit on sight
- Put away dirty dishes
- Open up the curtains, let sunlight in
- Wipe down bathrooms
- Close toilet lid
- Keep personal photos to a minimum. let the buyer visualize themselves at home.
- Remove scuff marks
- Keep driveways clear of vehicles, let the buyer appreciate the home without any obstacles in sight
- Do a quick sweep of the floors
- Empty trash cans

Chapter 3

REPAIRS, UPGRADES & ADDITIONS

When you are selling your property, there's always the doubt whether to invest money into the property or sell it as-is. There is no easy answer to this question, each sale is unique and should be analyzed based on its own weight. Try to be objective about it, and rationalize your decision based on costs vs profit.

Repairs
When you are ready to list your property, perform a self-inspection of your it. When we live in a home for many years, we start to develop blind spots; we notice that new leaky faucet in the kitchen, then we ignore it, and later we completely stop seeing it. Try to see your home as a buyer would for the first time. Make a list of any repairs or visual blemishes and put a priority value on them.

There's always a question of whether it's worth spending money on repairs and recouping it in the sale of your property. For large repairs, there is no general rule, each situation is different, and it should be carefully analyzed.

One way to make a decision easier is by repairing those items that are most obvious and will affect a buyers first impression. Take care of broken doors, holes or patches in the walls, missing tiles, leaky faucets, broken door knobs, etc. These repairs will make your home look liveable and solid, and this is what you want to convey to potential buyers.

The big-ticket items that are more expensive such as, heating and air conditioning, should consider the cost of replacing the units vs recouping those costs. If replacing the aging air conditioning unit will cost you $6000, you might get away by offering the buyer a credit of lower value at close of escrow. This avoids spending money up front and giving the buyers the option of spending this credit according to their priorities.

Upgrades
Should you make your property stand out above the rest of the competition. Once again recouping the costs invested should be one of the driving factors in your decision. Another factor to consider should be, how fast would this upgrade help you sell your property. Other external factors come in to play, are you in a buyers or sellers' market. In a sellers' market, buyers will often overlook aesthetics in their quest to get into a home, on the other hand in a buyers' market sellers need to find a way to make their homes stand out to have a chance of selling fast. Once again take a hard look at the financials and whether they make sense for you to invest in upgrades.

Additions
We keep hitting the same theme with additions, keep an eye on costs vs profit. There are times when adding an extra room, or an extra bathroom will be worth it. Ask your agent to run comparables using different scenarios. If adding an extra bedroom will bring you an additional $40,000 and the cost to do the room is $20,000 then it might be a good idea to invest on adding the extra bedroom.

Using licensed contractors or doing the work yourself

When it comes to doing big repairs or upgrades, it is recommended that you use licensed contractors. They might offer you transferable warranties that can carry on to the buyer, this minimizes potential liabilities or shift them to the contractors in case the work is defective. If you do the work yourself, be transparent, disclose it and let the buyer make a decision fully aware of this fact.

Chapter 4

CURB APPEAL

Curb appeal is the attractiveness of the exterior of a property when viewed from the street. This is the initial impression that the buyer has of your property. As a home seller you need to be aware of the buyers' perceptions and work towards creating a positive first impression. When you are selling your home and pondering improvement costs vs the valued added to your property, the following are simple tasks that you can do to increase the curb appeal of your home. Most of these tasks are easy to do and they will help sell your property faster and for a higher price.

- Exterior paint
- Paint front door
- Add front porch furniture, add a porch swing.
- Swap out your address house numbers for bigger, bolder numbers.
- Install flower window boxes and/or add flower beds around trees
- Replace your welcome mat or give it a good cleaning
- Freshen up exterior lighting fixtures.
- Repair large concrete walkway cracks
- Mow your lawn often

- Add a wooden picket fence: it provides a sense of privacy
- Keep water hose rolled up
- Paint garage door
- Polish doorknobs
- Paint or replace mailboxes
- Add outdoor ornaments: birdbaths, metal sculptures, windchimes, water fountains
- Pressure wash concrete pathways and driveways
- Clean the roof of any branches or leaves
- Replace missing roof tiles or shingles

Chapter 5

STAGING YOUR HOME

Home staging is decorating, rearranging furniture, use of lighting and finding the best use for each room in a home to sell it for top dollar and in the shortest amount of time.

Typically staging is used in vacant homes to make them more appealing to buyers, although it can also be used on occupied homes to better showcase the home. While home staging is similar to home decorating, the sole purpose of home staging is geared to improve the marketability of the home, get a higher sale price and reduce the time to sell. Staging a home will usually bring in more and better offers. Home sellers have different options when it comes to staging a home, they can go solo and decorate their home themselves or get a professional staging company to do it. The two most important factors to consider is cost and time. If the added value of the home justifies the staging cost, then it might be a good idea to stage the home. If you are going to use a staging company, keep a close tab on the costs. Many companies charge a fee for the initial staging and a monthly fee to cover the rental expenses of the furniture or artwork provided.

If you are interested in staging your home, but are put off by the high cost, you may hire a staging company to give you a list of suggestions to implement yourself. This will allow you to save on monthly expenses, while giving your home an edge over the competition.

Chapter 6

DISCLOSURES

Home sellers have an obligation to provide the buyer with legally required disclosures. The required disclosures vary from state to state, check with your local real estate agent to guide you.

Sellers will be better served by disclosing early any issues of the home with the buyers. This will avoid any delays or wasted time during the sale process, in case the buyer decides to cancel during the inspection period due to needed repairs.

As a general rule, sellers must disclose all material facts about the property. Material facts are those that might affect the decision making of a buyer. There are exceptions to this rule and every state has different specific disclosures.

Be aware that you need to disclose items that have already been corrected. For example, if the roof had a leak years ago, and you paid someone to repair it. Even though it was corrected, you need to disclose the fact that it leaked at one point in time, and it was corrected.

Disclosing does not mean that you need to repair or fix the

pending issues, it just means that you are making the buyer aware of it and he can use this information to make an appropriate buying decision.

If you are selling by owner, make sure you enlist the help of a Real Estate Attorney to assist you with proper disclosures.

Chapter 7

FAIR HOUSING

Fair Housing laws exists to guarantee the right to choose housing free from unlawful discrimination. There are Federal, State and Local Fair Housing laws designed to protect people from discrimination in housing rentals and sales.

Home sellers have an obligation and legal requirement under Fair Housing laws not to discriminate in the sale of their property on the basis of race, color, religion, gender, disability, familial status or national origin. Home sellers cannot instruct their representing broker to discriminate or screen potential buyers based upon these factors. In addition to these federal laws, sellers must adhere to state and/or local laws that might add additional protected classes not covered by federal laws. If you have doubts on what your rights, obligations and responsibilities are, you can visit www.hud.gov and/or visit your state real estate department webpage.

It is very important for home sellers to educate themselves on Fair Housing laws to avoid potential legal liabilities of intentional or accidental violations of Fair Housing laws.

Chapter 8

PRICING YOUR HOME

When it comes to real estate, location is king. Your local real estate trends are what matters most, and this will determine your pricing strategy. If you watch the news and see properties selling like pancakes in an adjoining city, do not expect your local neighborhood to follow identical selling patterns. Real estate trends are modified by local neighborhood factors. Keep an eye open on your local market to get an idea of how it compares to the market at large.

There are many ways to analyze market trends and you or your agent must be aware of what is the best way to gauge where your home stands against the competition.

Many home sellers arrive at a price, based solely on square footage of their home. If the neighbor's home was a 1200 square foot home and sold for $200,000 netting them $166.66 per square foot, they assume their 1600 square foot home is worth around $266,000 (1600X$166). When the time comes to list their home, many sellers push the agent to list their home based upon their own assumptions. Using price per foot may lead to underpriced or overpriced home listings. A better and more accurate method is to use comparables to arrive at a price point.

Home features and amenities will also determine how fast your property will sell and whether it justifies listing at a higher price. Common features that might shift a price point are homes with a pool, RV gate, garage, oversized lot, number of stories, irrigation rights, horse property, high ceilings, HOA, recent upgrades, repairs, etc. If you or your agent is able to perceive a pricing pattern, then you can adjust the price accordingly.

Price ranges are another way to analyze market trends, if the average days on the market for a metro area is 20 days. This means that in average, houses spend 20 days listed for sale before receiving and accepting an offer. This statistic will vary across different price ranges. It might be 10 days for properties under $200k; 25 days for properties in the $200k to $250K range and 50 days for properties listed from $250k to $350K. If you have a property looking to list for $325,000 you need to be aware of this kind of statistics, so you can have realistic expectations regarding the length of the sale process.

Absorption Rate
Ask your agent what the absorption rate is in your local market, this figure will give you a quick idea of the available supply of properties in the market vs the number of buyers. The absorption rate will help you determine if you are in a sellers or buyers' market. Use this information to create a pricing range and selling strategy.

Comparables (Comps)
Comparables (or comps) refers to properties with characteristics that are similar to a subject property whose value is being analyzed. Most agents use "comps" or comparables to get an approximate price point when listing a property. A comparable analysis uses properties located within the same or similar neighborhood, that are similar in size, year built, condition and features of the subject property. These comparables may include active listings, pending or sold listings. These comparables are not

only used by sellers, but also by buyers looking to verify they are paying a fair price for the property. Comparables should not be mistaken for appraisals or guarantees that the house will sell at that price. They are provided as a guide for the seller to make a decision regarding the price of the property.

Setting a price in your home is not exact science, every property is different and unique. A listing agent will make price suggestions based on comparables, experience and market trends, but the final decision rests on the home seller, he's the one that has the most vested interest on the final figure.

Pricing strategies

Once you arrive at a price range based on comparable properties or other method, you need to decide what will be the listing price. There are pros and cons for every option, and it's up to you to evaluate your needs against the market trends.

Price high

Listing your property at a high price has the benefit of selling for more profit, provided you get that special buyer that falls in love with your home. The downside is that a house with a higher price will get fewer showings, more scrutiny, and it might linger on the market unsold. A property that has been in the market for a long period of time, might get a stigma attached to it. Buyers will question why the house has been in the market for so long. In addition, a smart buyer's agent might use days on the market as a negotiating tool to drive the point that the house is not worth as much the seller thinks it is.

Price low

The benefits of pricing low are better odds of getting the property sold faster and getting multiple offers. The drawback of this strategy is the risk of leaving money on the table. It is worth noting that pricing low does not guarantee a bidding war, there are many factors besides price that will determine multiple offers.

There is no right or wrong selling strategy, it all comes down to sellers needs and motivation. The seller would be better served by keeping an open channel of communication with the listing agent to come up with an appropriate sales approach.

Strategy adjustments
There are times where you might do all your homework, cover all the bases, put it on the market and the home does not sell. Take a hard look at what are the possible reasons behind it and adjust your selling strategy.

Lots of showings, no offers
If your property is getting lots of showings, but you are not getting offers, get feedback from potential buyers. It could something simple such as the interior walls colors, and buyers can't visualize how it would look in a different color. Use the feedback to design a strategy to make it more appealing.

No showings & no offers
If your property is not getting any showings, this might mean that the price is too high, or curb appeal is lacking.

Getting offers & falling thru during escrow
If you are getting offers or contracts on your property, and they are being cancelled during course of escrow, identify, the root cause behind the cancellation and address those issues. Some possible reasons are appraisal contingency, inspection contingency, financing contingency, etc. Multiple cancellations due to the same issue, represent an obvious deeper look at this issue.

Chapter 9

TYPE OF LISTINGS

There are many options available when you are ready to sell your property. These are some of the most common ways to list your property. Some might appeal to you more than others, and each has its advantages and disadvantages.

Exclusive Right-to-Sell Listing
This is the listing agreement most commonly used by real estate agents. Under this agreement, the owner gives the real estate agent exclusive right to sell their property. In this agreement, the owner is responsible for paying the listing broker and the buyers' broker commissions. This contract does not allow the owner to sell their home by-owner, unless there are exceptions written within the listing agreement.

Open Listing
In an open listing, the owner may enter into non-exclusive agreements with more than one real estate broker. The owner is only responsible to pay commission to the broker that brings in a buyer. This type of listing may also allow the seller to sell by owner and avoid paying commissions.

Flat Fee listings

Flat fee listing is where a seller pays the listing agent a flat fee instead of a commission percentage to list their property and upload it to the MLS (Multiple Listing Service). Flat fee brokerages operate under different service models, some offer limited representation to the seller and others might offer services that closely aligns with a typical real estate brokerage. There are cons and pros with every flat fee broker, make sure you read the listing contract to avoid misunderstandings. Keep in mind that besides the flat fee payment, you might still need to pay the buyer's agent for bringing you a buyer, and that flat fee listing is no longer a flat fee, but rather flat fee plus buyer's agent commission.

FSBO (for sale by owner)

For sale by owners refers to those listings in which the owner sells their property without assistance by a real estate broker. There are multiple pros and cons about selling your home by owner. The biggest benefit is that home owners will not pay commission to sell their property. One of the disadvantages is a limited pool of buyers searching the FSBO market, and finding agents willing to work with a FSBO listing. An overlooked fact by FSBO sellers is that the MLS provides a pool of buyers that are pre-approved for financing, these buyers usually are shown only MLS listings by the representing agent. Additionally, there are many potential pitfalls when selling by owner, it is recommended to consult an attorney, so you can be aware of what are your legal obligations and to navigate the sales contract.

What can you negotiate in a listing contract?

If you are listing your property with a real estate agent, keep in mind that you can negotiate the listing contract terms. The listing contract is the document that establishes the terms under which the Real Estate

Broker is representing you. The following are some of the terms that you can negotiate.

- Commission: You can negotiate the commission that you will pay the listing agent and/or the buyers' agent. Keep in mind that offering a buyer's agent a lower commission, might discourage some buyer's agents from making an effort to show your property.
- Length of contract: If you think the length of the contract is too long, and you feel that you will be tied up into a listing contract, ask for a shorter period.
- Cancellation Terms: These terms address cancellation of listing agreement. Ask your agent to explain if there are any penalties or obligations for early cancellation.
- Lockboxes: If you don't feel comfortable having a lockbox in your property, tell your agent. Keep in mind, that lockboxes are one of the best tools to effectively market your property.

Each homeowner has different priorities, make sure you address them prior to signing the listing agreement. if you feel strongly about a certain term or clause within the contract, speak up and negotiate it.

Chapter 10

SHOWING YOUR PROPERTY

Your property is now listed for sale, now the goal is to get buyers to line up and make an offer. You need to show the best angle of your property and work with buyers' schedules to maximize the number of showings.

Sellers, STAY AWAY!!!!!!!
For many sellers it is tempting to stay home during showings; show potential buyers all the amenities and features of their home. They feel they are the best qualified to point out all the upgrades they have done to their property. The best advice for home sellers is to avoid being home whenever possible. Let buyers tour the home and envision themselves living in there. This might be their new home and it's essential to make them feel at ease.

If the buyers are being represented by a Real Estate Agent, they expect privacy, to be able to discuss the pros and cons of the property. The home buying experience is unique, buyers will constantly compare properties they have seen, they have become neighborhood home analysts and they want to have instant open discussions. These discussions are constructive in the overall sales process, and having the sellers at home, prevent this process to take place. Buyers won't be able to discuss the home, or talk openly about the price, without fear of insulting the seller or being overheard. Keep in mind, the more time buyers spend in the home, the more probabilities that they make an offer on it. The presence of the sellers will make buyers feel they are intruding and will keep their stay to a minimum.

There are times when leaving your home is not an option, in this case try to make yourself as invisible as possible, you might want to stay outside in the back patio or in a room. Be as inconspicuous as possible, let the buyers soak the beauty of your home in private.

Pets

This is a common and difficult issue, since many homeowners have pets that occupy a special place in their hearts. The ideal scenario is to have your home available for showings without having your pets roaming the property. Some people are nervous or afraid of dogs or other pets and their presence might prevent them from enjoying your home. An option is to have someone take care of your pets while your property is in the market. If this is not feasible, keep your pets under control or take them for a walk. Also keep in mind buyers might leave the door open while they are touring the home and let your pets out. Create a plan to work around your pets and showing appointments.

Advance notice

Buyer's agents will commonly go for the low hanging fruit. A buyer's agent will try to show those properties that are easier to show. Sellers that are flexible with appointment times will have better odds of having their property shown. A rental property with a tenant or a demanding seller, takes more effort from the agent to coordinate appointments that fit both tenants, and buyer's schedule. Whenever possible, be flexible with showing times and be accommodating to the buyer's schedule.

Showcase brochure

Create a brochure with all the amenities around your home. If you live in an HOA, list the parks, recreation centers, community pool, security or anything that might be perceived as a benefit. List all the grocery stores, gyms, other businesses close by, this will give a quick snapshot of the neighborhood to the new buyer. Make a copy and display in the counter tops, where the buyers can see it.

FSBOs

If you are a "sale by owner" seller, showing your home to potential buyers, usually means that you must be available at all times to answer any questions. If you need to point out the features and amenities of your home, create a written brochure, and let buyers wander and tour the home at their own pace, you can wait for them until they are done and answer any questions they might have. FSBO sellers need to be careful and verify buyers' credentials before any showings to avoid putting themselves at risk.

Safety tips

While most buyers are genuinely looking to purchase a home, there are people that are the exception and have other things in mind. The following are safety tips to follow when selling a property.

- Lock your valuables: Do not leave jewelry on the open, lock it in a secure place.
- Lock your guns, rifles etc.
- Put away mail and other documents that might make you vulnerable to identity theft.
- Put away medical prescriptions in a secure place
- Keep your computer off and password protected
- Install security cameras to monitor your property while you are away

Chapter 11

MARKETING YOUR PROPERTY

Marketing your property is essential to attract buyers, if you are selling by owner, do some research and decide which advertising platforms do you want to invest your time and money. There are many ways to market your property, each comes with its own cost. The following are the most common ways to market your property today.

MLS (Multiple Listing Service)
When it comes to marketing your property, the best option that you have at your disposal is the MLS. This is the place where engaged sellers and buyers meet. Buyer's agents will show properties only to those buyers that are serious and have had their income and credit analyzed by a mortgage lender.

Showing availability
It doesn't matter how well marketed your property is, or how many interested buyers you are able to attract, if you are not willing to show the home when the buyers want, then all that effort will be wasted. This cannot be overstated enough, accommodate the buyer whenever is possible. The use of lockboxes is one of the best ways to show your home, they are flexible and easy to use. Today's lockboxes keep a record of those agents that accessed your property, they provide a

level of accountability and, they allow the listing agent to gauge the interest level when buyers visit the property multiple times.

Open house

Whether you are selling by owner or through an agent, the use of open houses can be a useful marketing tool. Neighbors are frequent open house visitors and they become marketing ambassadors by discussing the amenities of your home with their friends and family.

Zillow/Realtor/Trulia

Most of the buyers that are on the fences waiting to buy, start looking at sites such as Zillow, Realtor, or Trulia. Advertising your property on these sites allows your property to be put in front of these potential new buyers, the downside is that many of these buyers have yet to line up financing and can turn out to be flaky buyers.

Social Media

There are many ways to advertise your property on social media sites, such as Facebook, Twitter, Instagram, using paid ads or organic ads. In Facebook there are many local groups, or niche interest groups where you can upload your property, results can be mixed, it's mostly trial and error until you reach an acceptable response rate.

Craigslist

Good old Craigslist is still a good place to advertise your property for sale. Although it doesn't have the traffic that it used to have, and the younger generation is pivoting away from it, there is still a large segment of the population that still uses Craigslist as their main online marketplace.

Newspapers/Magazines

Newspapers and magazines are becoming less and less relevant, but there are people that are still faithful and consistent readers of paper news. Before advertising on a magazine or newspaper, make sure you understand which niche audience they are serving and whether your property might appeal to them.

These are just a few ways that you can market your property, some of these apply to FSBO's, others to agent listings. When your property is on the market, you need to put on your salesman's cap. Bring up the topic of your property for sale in your everyday conversations, you never know who's in the market for a new home.

Chapter 12

CHOOSING AN OFFER

If you are selling with a real estate agent, ask them for a copy of the standard contract beforehand so you can study it. When you receive an offer, keep all options on the table. If it meets your demands, you can accept it. If the offer is close to what you are looking for, you can write a counter offer to modify those terms that you don't agree with. If the initial offer is not close to your ballpark figure you can reject it or probe the buyer to see gauge his interest.

Keep your priorities at view

If you are looking to get the most money out of your property, choosing an offer based only on monetary amount would be a good option. If you are looking for an expedited closing, a cash offer might be a better alternative, even though it might be a lower offer. If your kids are in school and you want them to finish their school year before moving out, then an extended closing might be your best fit.

Multiple offers

If you receive multiple offers, compare them based on monetary value, probabilities of successfully closing and other additional factors that are important to you. Selecting an offer based only on highest price comes with its own risk. If the property does not appraise for the purchase price, the buyer might walk rather than pay over market price. Have a plan in mind for the appraisal contingency, in case you choose the highest offer and appraisal comes in low.

Don't take it personal
Selling your home is an emotional life event. Sellers might perceive a low offer as a personal slight, be prepared for these offers. Do not be offended, just consider it part of the negotiation. Keep in mind that only an interested buyer will take the time to write up an offer.

Analyze the terms of the offer
Each purchase offer is different, evaluate what the buyer is offering and respond accordingly. The following are some of the most common terms negotiated.
- Price
- Earnest money amount
- Close of escrow
- Contingencies
- Inspection period
- Personal property included
- Home warranty
- Sellers concessions
- Repairs
- Time of possession

Be imaginative
Price is not everything in a purchase offer, look for ways to reach an agreement with the buyer. Receiving an offer is not the end game, it is just the start.

Chapter 13

UNDERSTANDING THE CONTRACT

Typically, real estate agents use a standardized contract that is meant to protect buyers and sellers from using ambiguous language. While a standard has pre-printed terms, it does not mean that it can't be modified. Educate yourself about the terms, it will make it easier to understand the consequences of each of the terms and conditions.

Offer

The first thing most sellers will look at, it's the purchase offer price. While this section is one of the most important items on a purchase offer, it is not the only thing that you need to keep in mind. When multiple offers are received, take a look at other factors such as financing and sellers' concessions. For a seller looking to sell fast, an all cash offer might be a better alternative than a higher offer using financing.

Counteroffer

A counteroffer is an alternative offer to the original offer. It implies a rejection of the original offer. When you receive an offer, you can accept it as written, reject it or send a counter offer. Be aware that when you decide to counter an offer, you are basically rejecting the offer received. The main purpose of a counteroffer is to find a common agreement, that satisfies both buyer and seller.

Accepted contract

An accepted contract or executed contract is when both buyer and seller have agreed and signed the purchase offer that specifies price and terms of sale for the subject property. It will have specific language to clarify earnest money, financing, deadlines, inspections, cure periods, remedies and any other items or clauses added.

Earnest Money

Earnest money is a deposit by the buyers as a show of good faith, that they are genuinely interested in purchasing the property. The buyers are putting some skin in the game, in order to go thru with the sales process. The earnest money is usually deposited with an escrow company, that will serve as an independent neutral third party. In case the sale is canceled, and the ownership of the earnest money is in question, the escrow company will decide who keeps the earnest money based upon the terms of the contract

Financing

This section will specify the kind of financing being used, FHA, VA or Conventional. If the buyer includes an approval from his lender, examine the approval letter for the financing terms. If possible talk to the lender to gauge the strength of the buyer's ability to obtain financing.

Sellers concessions

This section specifies buyer's requests to the seller. If the buyer is asking the seller for help with closing costs, this is where you will find the details. Keep track of seller's concessions, it will have a direct impact on the amount of money that goes into the sellers' pocket.

Inspections

The inspection contingency allows the buyer a determined time period to perform inspections that he/she considers essential. These inspections may include, physical inspection of the property, presence of radon, termite, foundation, lead based paint, neighborhood area, zoning, HOA regulations. These are just a small sample of possible specific inspections that may be performed by the buyer. If the buyer is dissatisfied with the inspection, he may send a disapproval document to the seller with an option to cancel, option to proceed with the sale or give the seller an option to repair or remedy the items disapproved. The seller in turn may decide to repair the items requested, do a partial repair or just decline to do any repairs. At this point the ball is back in the buyer's court, if the seller decides not to do a full repair of the items, then the buyer may cancel or proceed with the sale.

Sellers response to buyers' inspection requests
When the seller gets a buyer's inspection request from the seller asking for repairs, he has options.
- Seller agrees to perform all repairs requested. The sale proceeds as before.
- Seller agrees to perform partial repairs. Since the seller is not agreeing to repair all the items requested, the buyer may proceed or cancel the contract. Talk to the buyer before sending the response, find out what items he considers deal breakers and work with this information.
- Seller does not agree to perform any repairs. The buyer at this point may cancel or proceed with the sale without any repairs.
- Seller agrees to provide a credit at close of escrow in lieu of repairs. This is a good option, when the property needs costly repairs. It will help the owner comply with buyers' requests and avoid spending money that he may not have.

This is one of the most stressful phases of the selling process for the seller. Do not take the repair requests personal, work with the buyer to find a common ground on those repairs the buyer considers critical.

Personal property

This is one of the most common contract items, where misunderstanding occurs. Make it clear on the contract what personal items are included in the sale. Let your listing agent know, so he adds it into the MLS listing details. Anything that is considered a fixture; permanently attached to the property is implicitly included in the sale. Many times, sellers are not aware of this, and they will assume that their new gas stove is not included on the sale. The inclusions of comments on the MLS listing attesting to personal property excluded or included in the sale, must also be written within the contract to be enforceable. Stating your intentions clearly, will help in avoiding buyer and seller misunderstandings.

Extensions

A purchase contract has many different deadlines that call for certain events to take place, these deadlines may be extended by the agreement of both buyer and seller. Often close of escrow is delayed due the buyer's lender not ready to fund the loan at the agreed time, the seller may at this time start cancellation process or give the buyer an extension to give him enough time to get the loan. This extension allows the buyer extra time to get his loan approved. The disadvantage for the seller is that during this extra time, the seller might incur additional expenses due to the delayed closing. One way to alleviate these extra expenses on the seller is to ask for a portion, or all of the earnest money to become non-refundable as a condition of giving the buyer an extension. This option should be analyzed in the context of the market at large. In a sellers' market, the buyer might be motivated to accept it, on a buyers' market, it might not work as well.

Contingencies

A contingency clause is a condition or action that must be met, for the purchase contract to be binding. If those conditions are not met, it might give the seller or buyer a way out of the contract without suffering any monetary or legal damages. Purchase contracts used by real estate agents are standardized to cover the most common contingencies, but the inclusion, modification or removal of contingencies are negotiable. The buyer may add contingencies to the contract or the seller may ask to remove certain contingencies. The contingencies found on standardized contracts may change from state to state. Get familiarized with them and how they affect the contract. The following are some of the most common contingencies found in a purchase contract.

Inspection contingency
Inspection contingency defines a time period where the buyer is entitled to have a home inspector check the condition of the property. The scope of the inspection might not be limited to the physical condition of the home, but also include the neighborhood, insurance claims against the home, title commitment or other material facts that might be of interest to the buyer. If the buyer has objections to the results of the inspection, he may cancel or opt to give the seller a chance to remedy the disapproved items.

Loan contingency
Loan contingencies are put in place to favor the buyer in case he does not qualify for a mortgage loan at predetermined terms. If the buyer is not able to qualify for the loan, then he might have the option to cancel the contract at that time, without forfeiting earnest money deposit or suffering other monetary or legal damages.

Appraisal contingency
This contingency is put in place to prevent the buyer from overpaying for a property or not being able to obtain a loan for the full amount of the contract price. For example, if the agreed purchase price is

$200,000 and the appraisal is 190,000 then the buyer may opt to cancel the contract based upon this contingency.

Other contingencies

One of most common contingencies is the buyer making the purchase of a home contingent upon the finalized sale of their own home. In this case the buyer might be using the proceeds from the sale of their property, towards their new home. The buyer's failure to sell their property will allow them to withdraw from the contract of the home they were buying without any damages.

There are many kinds of contingencies, and every contract is written different. Make sure you take the time to understand the type of contingencies clauses included in the contract.

Deadlines

"Time is of the Essence" clause is usually included in a purchase contract to denote the importance of time. The contract includes various deadlines that determine the time of certain conditions to be met. The following are common deadlines in a Real Estate contract.

1. Offer or counter offer acceptance
2. Earnest money to be deposited with escrow company
3. Delivery of seller property disclosures to buyer
4. Inspection period
5. Close of escrow

Cure period

A cure period is a time period specified in the contract to allow a breaching party to correct or remedy the items in question.

Remedies

If the buyer or seller are in breach of contract, there might be a number of options available for the affected party. These options depend on the specific language in the contract. If the buyer is in breach of contract, the seller may write a cure period notice, demand earnest money, sue the buyer for damages, attend mediation, or demand specific performance of the contract. Every and contract is different, make sure to understand what your options are.

Chapter 14

CONDOMINIUM SALES

One of the biggest mistakes made when selling a condominium is assuming that is the same process as selling a single family detached home. The process might be similar, but not the same, especially when it comes to lending guidelines. If you are a condominium owner looking to sell, you need to educate yourself on the process and unique challenges of condominium selling.
Follow the following tips to improve your odds of successfully selling your condominium

1. **Get it ready**
- Make it look more spacious, declutter, pack away large items. Condominiums are usually smaller than a home and they can look cramped when occupied. Go through every single storage space in your condominium and declutter. In the kitchen cabinets, pack away all those large pots and pans, go through the pantry and make sure it looks tidy. If possible pack away all those food items that you can live without, while your condominium is on the market. If you have the financial means, rent a storage unit to store all those packed boxes.

- Patch, paint and repair all that is needed. Keep in mind that your main competitors will be almost identical units and you need to make sure you have an edge over the rest of them.
- Stage it, once again you need to make sure your condominium stands out against the competition.
- Keep it clean and ready to show at any time
- Try to accommodate showing requests as much as possible. Having restrictions on showing availability is one of the worst mistakes when selling a property. Real estate agents usually follow a scheduled tour to show properties to buyers, if you are not available, they might not come back to show your property.

2. **Know the HOA (Home Owners Association) rules and regulations**
   - Buyers will need to take a look at HOA rules as part of the required disclosures, get an early jump and have them available at the start of the process. This will prevent delayed closings or cancelled sales due to buyers disapproving the HOA rules.
   - Have HOA name, number, address and email address at hand to provide as requested.
   - Provide buyer with HOA fees, assessments early on.

3. **Investigate if your condominium is warrantable and meets federal lending criteria of Freddie Mac and/or Fannie Mae.**

   Buyer financing is one of the biggest differences between selling a home vs selling a condominium. If your condominium is deemed not warrantable, your pool of buyers will shrink, those buyers approved for FHA, VA and some conventional loans will not be able to buy your condominium.

Call your HOA or a lender to see if your condominium is considered warrantable.

The following factors may affect warrantability

- Projects where single entity owns more than a certain percentage of total number of condominiums
- Projects that are part of a Hotel, Resort or timeshare
- Projects where certain percentage of total spaces are used for non-residential or commercial purposes
- Projects that represent legal, but non-conforming use of land (zoning issue)
- Percentage of condominiums with FHA loans
- Percentage of nonowner occupied condominiums
- HOA cannot be named in any current lawsuits

Typically mortgages for condominiums are more expensive than single family homes. This is due to the fact that a condominium is subject to risk factors that are beyond the borrowers control. To account for this risk, banks might require larger down payments and higher interest rates. It is a good idea to investigate all you can about your condominium complex, before putting your condominium in the market. FHA, VA and Conventional guidelines might change, keep up with the latest updates. This information will be helpful in coming up with a sales strategy. If your condominium is approved for conventional, or FHA financing, include it in your marketing materials or MLS description.

4. **Pricing your condominium**

The process for pricing your condominium is similar to home sales. Run a comparable analysis of active, pending and sold listings in your condominium complex and make adjustment based on other factors such as square footage, amenities, location within the complex, views, etc. If you are selling with a real estate agent ask him for absorption rate on the condominium market, this will provide you with a better perspective on the time that it takes to sell a condominium in your area.

5. **Be ready for inspections**
    - Check inside plumbing for leaks
    - Check all electrical outlets and fans work
    - Check Air conditioning and Heating
    - Check for missing floor tiles
    - Check appliances are in working condition.

When selling your condominium, being proactive pays off, cooperate with buyers and make their lives easier by having everything ready. This will improve your chances of having a smooth selling process of your condominium.

Chapter 15

LAND SALES

First and most important question to answer, what is the reason behind your desire to sell. Do you want to cash out your investment, do you need to sell due to personal or financial circumstances, or did you realized that building your dream home will be more expensive than you expected. Whatever your reason, take that into account when putting up your land for sale and execute a sale strategy that fits your situation.

Who buys land?
Identifying potential buyers will give you a better perspective on the listing price and how fast it might sell. If you are selling a land in the middle of nowhere, no utilities in place and a long way from civilization, chances are that buyers looking to build immediately will be removed from your pool of buyers. You may classify the buyers as follow and keep this in mind when listing it.
- Developers: They might be looking to sit on the land, or build right away, subdivide or assemble lots.
- Speculators: They are willing to sit on the lot and waiting for it to appreciate in value.
- Buyers looking to build short term: This type of buyer want to close the sale, and immediately start working on their plans to build. They want to buy a lot that is as ready-to-build as

possible. Make sure you do your due diligence as a seller to make your lot more enticing for buyers to send you an offer.
- Buyers looking to build long term: They have long term plans for the property, but are not in a rush to buy.

Land sales vs home sales

The real estate market for land is different from the housing market. The pool of buyers is smaller and it is harder to qualify for financing. Generally, when financing land, it will require a higher down payment and higher interest rates when compared to home mortgages. If you are using a real estate agent to sell your land, make sure you ask what the current trends in land sales are. The residential housing trends might not equate to land sales. Be aware of these trends and take it into consideration when pricing the land, it might make the difference in getting it sold fast.

Prepare the land for sale

Curb appeal has a more tangible feel for homes than land, but there are ways you can increase the curb appeal of land. First impression matters and having a lot of land that looks ready to build will bring in more buyers to the table. You need to weight the cost, and time involved in repairs of modifications against the value added to the land.

Clean the trash

Take the time to keep your lot free and clear of debris, keep weeds to a minimum and trim bushes and trees, remove any fallen branches.

Fix the gates

Make sure the gates open and close properly and there are working locking mechanisms. It is frustrating for buyers to make the drive to see your land, only to be met with a gate that doesn't allow a car to pass through.

Repair fences
Do an inspection and repair those sections needing attention.

Clean up the buildings or structures
Do a quick cleaning of existing structures or buildings, it will make it easier for the buyer to visualize its potential.

Eliminate potential legal hurdles
Taking a proactive approach and eliminating any potential issues concerning the property, it will help you attract more buyers, avoid delays in closing the sale or outright cancellations.

Legal Access / Easements
Make sure you have recorded legal access to the property. Unrecorded easements might be enforceable but more difficult to enforce than recorded easements. A property with recorded easements granting ingress and egress access is more appealing than one with unrecorded access. If your lot has unrecorded easements, talk to a Real Estate Attorney to see what your options are.

Boundary lines
Do a survey to verify the boundary lines for the property. Perform a survey prior to listing the land, to give the buyer clear landmarks of the boundary lines.

Encroachments
Are you aware of any encroachments from your neighbors, take care of this issue beforehand, it will avoid delays during escrow.

Liens
Prevent any delays in the sale of your property, do a title search on

your property and check for any liens or encumbrances that may affect transfer of clear title.

Assessments
Are there any unpaid assessments, make sure you have a plan to take care of them.

Zoning restrictions
If the property is an area with zoning restrictions, disclose early to avoid delays or cancellations during the inspection period. .

Flood zone
Is your property partially or fully located in a flood zone? Flood zones are geographic areas that the FEMA (Federal Emergency Management Agency) has defined according to varying levels of flood risk. Property in a flood zone might be subject to higher insurance rates and/or stricter building requirements to mitigate the flooding risks.

Utilities
The value of land depends on many factors besides location; having utilities in place adds to the value. Investigate which utilities are serving your property and keep a list of the phone numbers for each utility company to share with the buyer. Weigh the cost of running utilities to your property vs the value added to it.

Sewer
Does the property already has a connection ready to be tapped on property, or does it need a sewer pipe to be run.

Septic
Does the property has septic system in place? If it does not, have you done a percolation test to see if you can install a septic system. If a

property fails the percolation test, it might imply that a septic system won't be approved and consequently a home won't be approved to build.

Water
How is your property served with water, are you able to tap into city water, is it delivered by truck or does it have its own water well?

Water well
Having service records and a working water pump will make the sale easier.

Electricity
Does your property has electricity on site? If not, do you know the cost of running a line to your property.

Phone or Cable
For many buyers the ability to have video and internet at home will weigh heavily in their buying decision. Factor this when setting the price.

Adding value to the property
You might be able to add value to your property by investigating about the allowed and/or potential uses for it.

Irrigation rights
Does your property have irrigation rights; make sure to emphasize it on your marketing brochures.

Horse property
Horse property is land that is suited for horses, this type of property is highly desirable by many buyers. When buying or selling horse property do not make assumptions about the property privileges.

Check with the city or county and verify that you are allowed to have horses on it.

Commercial zoning
Does the property borders a well traversed road, investigate with proper authorities about all potential uses of the property.

Subdividing land
Subdividing your land into smaller lots it's an option that might help you sell it faster and at a higher price. You need to weight the costs involved in subdividing it vs the potential gains. If you decide to go this route, talk to a Real estate attorney to guide you in the process of subdividing land.

Unincorporated areas
A property located in an unincorporated area has its pros and cons. An advantage might be that the property might not be limited by zoning restrictions as those in incorporated areas. A disadvantage could be the lack of services available, such as fire department that incorporated areas might enjoy. This type of property might be enticing for some buyers, while it might be a negative for others.

Pricing your property
A Real estate agent should be able to help you with pricing your property by using comparable land properties similar in size and amenities as your property. All the previous factors might affect the value of your property, adjust accordingly to find a price range that will fit your needs. If the land is unique or there are no comparables available, get an appraisal to get a better value of your land. Keep in mind the market trends specific to land, to reach a price range for your property.

Carry back loan

This is a loan made by a seller to the buyer to finance full or part of the purchase price at an agreed interest rate. Offering carry back financing will increase the number of buyers interested in your property. Seller carry back has its advantages and risks. An advantage is that you have a steady stream of interest income. The main risk is buyer defaulting on the loan. Land sellers interested in offering carry back financing should consult a real estate attorney to advise them in the process and risks involved.

For sale by owners (FSBO)

Selling by owner has its pros and cons; it can net you more money in your pocket, but getting an offer might be more difficult since the pool of buyers will be smaller than one listed with a real estate agent. An agent has many marketing tools at his disposal, the best tool to maximize exposure of your property is the MLS (Multiple Listing Service). This tool is available to agents that belong to this association. Another issue is that many buyers feel more secure if the transaction is handled by a real estate agent. If you are selling by owner, do your homework, talk to a Real Estate Attorney to answer the questions you may have and make sure to educate yourself about your legal obligations.

Chapter 16

SELLING AND BUYING SIMULTANEOUSLY

Whenever you are buying and selling a home at the same time, it is essential that you are aware of your local real estate trends. Ask your real estate agent if you are in a seller's market, buyer's market or balanced market. The state of the market dictates the best option to buy and sell simultaneously.

Selling first & Buying later
If you are looking for a stress-free way to sell your home and buy another one, this is the best way to do it. Sell your home, then do a short-term rental while you look for a new home. You will not be rushed to selling your property under a certain period of time, or finding a home before you close on the sale of your property. There are disadvantages with this option, in a sellers' market every month that goes by, could potentially mean home price increases. Every month that you spend on the sidelines, the proceeds from the sale of your property will afford less and less real estate.

On the contrary, if you are in a buyers' market, you will find plenty of homes. There's no rush to buy, since homes are not appreciating. Additionally, having cash on hand will give you an upper hand when you put an offer on a property.

Buying first & Selling later
The disadvantage of this option is that you might be stuck with two mortgages while you find a buyer for your home. If you are able to afford both mortgages, this is good option to buy and sell your home. If you are in a sellers' market, the time needed to sell should be minimal. If you are on a buyers' market, the large inventory of homes available on the market means that either your property will take a long time to sell or you will need to set your price low in order to move it fast.

Buying & Selling at the same time
Selling a home, while buying another one at the same time is a very common practice, but it needs patience, strategy and a bit of luck for everything to happen without delays. In a normal sale there are many factors that may cause a sale to fall through. When you are buying and selling at the same time, these factors are doubled and the odds of the contract falling through as well.

One of the best ways to sell your property and buy another is to list your property first, start looking at homes and be ready to put an offer on your dream home as soon as you get a purchase offer on yours. The reasoning behind it, is that most sellers will only take an offer contingent on the buyer selling their home, if the buyer's home is already listed and has a purchase contract on it.

If you are adamant on selling your home only if you are able to find one to buy, put a contingency clause stating sale of your property is contingent upon finding your next home and successfully closing on it. Including this contingency in the purchase contract will protect your earnest money. If the sale of your home fails to close, you have the option to cancel on the purchase and get the earnest money refunded.

Receiving an offer with a sale contingency

If you receive an offer with a selling contingency, do some digging before accepting it. Verify the buyer's home is already under contract. Ask for permission to speak to the lender handling the mortgage application for the buyer of the buyer's home. In this case both sales are dependent on the first buyer being able to close successfully. As an indirect party to that transaction, ask to be notified of any updates in the buyer's ability and willingness to close.

Chapter 17

SELLER VS BUYER'S MARKET

Real estate is like any other economic market, it is based on supply and demand. Stay on top of real estate news to see what kind of market your neighborhood is in.

Balanced market
A balanced market is when the number of buyers is fairly equal to the number of buyers. Housing Inventory supply will vary from three to six months.

Sellers' market
In a sellers' market, the number of buyers outnumber the houses available for sale. Inventory supply levels are typically less than three months. Bidding wars are common due to the shortage of inventory. In this market, sellers enjoy the high ground in the negotiations. They may demand full price offers, zero concessions, removal of appraisal contingency or decline to do any repairs.

Buyers' market
In a buyers' market the number of properties for sale outnumber the number of buyers. Properties linger in the market for long time periods, inventory supply levels typically exceed six months. In this

market buyers become choosy, demanding and expect sellers to be flexible on price and concessions.

If you are not sure what is the state of your local real estate market, ask your agent. He should be able to identify it for you, and with this information you can create a selling strategy. When you are analyzing the market try to break down the market into segments that are similar to the price range, location and type of property that you are selling. You might see a market with less than three months inventory in single family detached homes, and at the same time have land sales with supply inventory levels approaching two years.

Chapter 18

WHY MY PROPERTY DID NOT SELL?

This is the million-dollar question, every property is different, every market is different and there are a multitude of factors involved. Finding out why your property is not selling or did not sell, takes a little bit of research. If your property did not sell or has been lagging in the market for a long period of time, you need to be honest in your analysis. The following are simple steps to help you narrow down the possible causes.

Is the property getting any showings?
If you are not getting any showings, you have three main causes, poor marketing, curb appeal or price is too high.

If your property is listed in the MLS, make sure all features of the home are mentioned in the listing. The MLS is the biggest marketing tool available for real estate agents, showcase the features of your property in this platform and include plenty of photos.

Curb appeal is your opportunity to make a first impression, when buyers come see your home, they will take a quick look at the outside and decide whether to take a closer look or go on to the next home.

The third factor is price, if your house is overpriced it will not make the buyer's home tour list. Ask your agent to run comparables again and adjust your pricing point accordingly.

Another factor could be commission offered to buyer's agent, if you are offering a low commission compensation to the buyer's agent, it might discourage those agents from making an effort to show your property. They might place your home at the end of the list and show it only after the agent has exhausted all the other options.

Are you getting interest, but no showings?
If you or your agent are getting calls inquiring about the property, but they are not following up with actual showings, possible issues might be showing availability or curb appeal. Accommodate buyers requested showing times as much as possible.

Are you getting showings, but no offers?
The property might be priced comparable to similar properties, but on a closer look the other properties might be in better shape or it could be something inside that is turning the buyers off. Keep in mind that buyers become neighborhood experts while they are house shopping, and if they are touring your home and not sending you an offer, there might be a reason behind it. Ask your agent to get feedback from buyers, it could be something trivial and simple that is keeping buyers from taking the next step.

Are you getting offers, but no contracts?
If you have buyers willing to invest their time in writing up an offer, only to back out during the negotiations; go back and analyze why are they backing out and modify your strategy. It could be that you are being inflexible during the negotiations, of maybe there's a glut of properties available where the buyers are cherry picking the best

among them and having trouble committing to one property. Be objective in how you approach your analysis and find possible causes why you are not able to secure a contract.

Are you going under contract, but keeps falling out of escrow?
Ask yourself why the contracts are falling out, is it because of the buyer's inability to secure funding; if so, try vetting your buyers more carefully by calling the buyer's lender before accepting an offer.

If the contracts are falling out due to a contingency that is under your control, then you might be able to correct it. If the contract is falling out due to the appraisal contingency, that means the market does not agree with your personal assertion of value, you might have to wait for that special buyer to fall in love with your home and is willing to pay above market price. If it is falling out during the inspection period, then you have options available; be very open and upfront about possible issues, this will keep the buyer's expectations aligned with the condition of the property. Another option is to repair those items in question, or offer credit to the buyer at closing, so they can fix it up themselves. The advantage of offering credit at closing is that you won't be spending money on repairs without any guarantees the transaction will close. By offering the buyer credit you will only pay if the transaction closes.

Many sellers have their own perceptions of the real estate market based on what they see in the news, but when it comes to selling your home, keep in mind that real estate is local. Ask your real estate agent what the market trends are based in geographical location, type of properties and price segmentation. When searching for possible issues preventing the sale of your properties, put yourself in the buyer's shoes, be critical and objective. Think of any issues or factors that would discourage the buyer from buying your home.

Glossary

1031 exchange
A 1031 exchange allows an investor to sell a property and reinvest the proceeds in a new property, while deferring all capital gain taxes.

Absorption rate
Rate at which homes or land sell in a geographical market over a specific period of time. It is calculated by dividing number of properties sold during this period by the total number of properties currently for sale.

Accompanied showings
Those showings where the listing agent must accompany an agent and his or her clients when viewing a listing.

Real Estate Agent
The licensed real estate salesperson or broker who represents buyers or sellers.

Amendment
A change either to alter, add to, or correct part of an agreement without changing the principal idea or essence

ALTA
American Land Title Association. Organization composed of title insurance firms which sets standards for the industry including title insurance policy forms used on a national basis

Appraisal

An estimate of value of property resulting from analysis of facts about the property by a licensed appraiser. An opinion of value at a specific point in time.

Appreciation
Increase in the value of a property over a period of time.

Arm's length transaction
Transaction between buyer and seller, where each party negotiates, and act based on their self-interest.

"As-is" Sale
A contract or offer clause stating that the seller will not repair or correct any problems with the property.

Assessor Parcel Number
(APN) It is a distinctive number assigned to each parcel of land by county tax assessor.

Back on market (BOM)
When a property or listing is placed back on the market after being removed from the market recently.

Back-up offer
When an offer is accepted contingent on the fall through or voiding of an accepted first offer on a property.

Breach of contract
Failure to perform a contract, in whole or part.

Buyer's Agent
Licensed real estate agent who represents the buyer in a transaction.

Close of escrow
The date the documents are recorded, and title passes from Seller to Buyer.

Closing costs
Expenses, fees, prepayments associated with purchase and sale of a property.

Cloud on title
An irregularity, possible claim, or encumbrance which, if valid, would affect or impair the title.

CLUE (CLUE REPORT)
CLUE (Comprehensive Loss Underwriting Exchange) is the insurance industry's national database that assigns individuals a risk score. CLUE also has an electronic file of a property's insurance history. These files are accessible by insurance companies nationally. These files could impact the ability to sell property as they might contain information that a prospective buyer might find objectionable, and in some cases not even insurable.

Commission
The compensation paid to the listing brokerage by the seller for selling the property. A buyer agency agreement may require the buyer to pay a commission to his or her agent.

Comparative market analysis (also known as Comps)
A study done by real estate sales agents and brokers using active, pending, and sold comparable properties to estimate a listing price for a property.

Covenants, Conditions and Restrictions

Commonly called "CC & R's" the term usually refers to a written recorded declaration which sets forth certain covenants, conditions restrictions, rules or regulations placed on a group of residential properties, condominiums by a builder, developer, neighborhood association or homeowner's association.

Curb appeal
The visual impact a property projects from the street.

Days on market
The number of days a property has been on the market.

DOM
Days on market.

Down payment
The amount of cash put toward a purchase by the borrower.

Dual agent
A state-licensed individual who represents the seller and the buyer in a single transaction.

Earnest money deposit
The money given to the seller at the time the offer is made as a sign of the buyer's good faith.

Easement
A right held by a person to enjoy or make limited use of another's real property.

Egress
The right to a path or right-of-way over a property, that allows a person to leave or go away from his own real estate.

Encroachment
The extension of a structure from the real estate to which it belongs across a boundary line and onto adjoining property.

Encumbrance
A claim, right or lien upon the title to real estate, held by someone other than the real estate owner.

Escrow account for real estate taxes and insurance
An account into which borrowers pay monthly prorations for real estate taxes and property insurance.

Exclusions
Fixtures or personal property that are excluded from the contract or offer to purchase.

Expired (listing)
A property listing that has expired per the terms of the listing agreement.

Fee simple
A form of property ownership where the owner has the right to use and dispose of property at will.

FHA
Federal Housing Administration.

Fixture
Personal property that has become part of the property through permanent attachment.

Flat fee

A predetermined amount of compensation received or paid for a specific service in a real estate transaction.

For sale by owner (FSBO)
A property that is for sale by the owner of the property, without using a real estate agent to represent him in the sale.

Foreclosure
A legal proceeding for the collection of real estate mortgages and other types of liens on real estate, which results in cutting off the right to redeem the mortgaged property and usually involves a judicial sale of the property to pay the mortgage debt.

Gift letter
A letter to a lender stating that a gift of cash has been made to the buyer(s) and that the person gifting the cash to the buyer is not expecting the gift to be repaid. The exact wording of the gift letter should be requested of the lender.

Ingress
The right or permission to enter; right-of-way to entry across adjoining land.

Lien
The liability of real estate as security for payment of a debt. Such liability may be created by contract, such as a mortgage, or by operation of law, such as a mechanics lien.

Lis Pendens
A pending lawsuit. A lis pendens notice is legal notice to the world that a lawsuit is pending.

Listing agent
The real estate sales agent that is representing the sellers and their property, through a listing agreement.

Loan closing costs
The costs a lender charges to close a borrower's loan. These costs vary from lender to lender and from market to market.

Loan commitment
A written document stating that the mortgage company has agreed to lend the borrower a specific amount of money at a specific interest rate for a specific period of time. The loan commitment may also contain conditions upon which the loan commitment is based.

Lockbox
A tool that allows secure storage of property keys on the premises for agent use. A combo uses a rotating dial to gain access with a combination; a Supra® (electronic lockbox or ELB) features a keypad.

Mechanics lien
A lien on real estate, created by operation of law, which secures the payment of debts due to persons who perform labor or services or furnish materials incident to the construction of buildings and improvements on the real estate.

Multiple Offers
More than one buyer broker presents an offer on one property where the offers are negotiated at the same time.

Off market
A property listing that has been removed from the sale inventory in a

market. A property can be temporarily or permanently off market.

Sale Pending
A real estate contract that has been accepted on a property, but the transaction has not closed.

Purchase Offer
When a buyer proposes certain terms and presents these terms to the seller

Quit Claim Deed
A deed that does not imply the grantor holds title, but which surrenders and gives to the grantee any possible interest or rights that the grantor may have in the property.

Temporarily off market (TOM)
A listed property that is taken off the market due to illness, travel, repairs, and so on.

Under contract
A property that has an accepted real estate contract between seller and buyer.

VA
U.S. Department of Veterans Affairs.

VA Loan Guarantee
A guarantee on a mortgage amount backed by the U.S. Department of Veterans Affairs.

Walk-through
A showing before closing or escrow that permits the buyers one final tour of the property they are purchasing.

ABOUT THE AUTHOR

My name is Luis Carrasco. I'm a licensed Real Estate agent in Arizona since 2005. I'm currently working with Re/Max Professionals, one of the best real estate brokerages in Arizona. I have also been licensed in Colorado with Your Castle Real Estate. I love working in real estate and helping people navigate one of the biggest decisions in their lives. I consider my job not only helping my clients selling or buying their homes, but also educating them in the process. I'm fluent in English and Spanish. I am able to assist in the unique language challenges that a Spanish speaking client encounters when buying or selling a home.

I hope you enjoyed the book and become a better home seller, a better investor, better negotiator or a better home buyer.

If you are looking to sell or buy a property in Arizona, please contact me

Luis Carrasco

Re/Max Professionals

602-643-8224

WWW.SOLDBYCARRASCO.COM

www.ingramcontent.com/pod-product-compliance
Lightning Source LLC
Chambersburg PA
CBHW070925220526
45469CB00015B/2383